Cairo by Camel

Written by Janine Scott
Photography by Jason Lauré

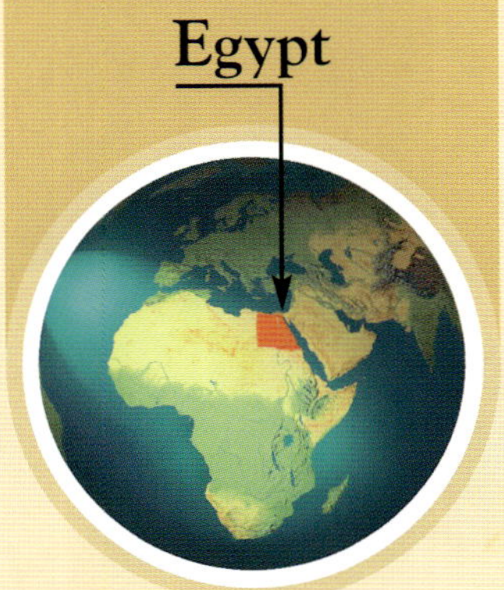

Meher lives in the busy city of Cairo. His father shows tourists the ancient wonders of Cairo by camel. He has always taught Meher to respect the past. Meher loves to listen to his father tell the tourists stories about old and new Egypt.

respect to place a high value on something

Contents

Cairo by Camel

Meher lives in Egypt, the land of pyramids, markets, and feluccas. Like many people in Egypt, Meher's father works in the tourist industry. He takes tourists on sightseeing trips on his camels. Tourists play an important role in the life of Cairo. People from all around the world come to visit the pyramids, the Great Sphinx, and the many other relics and wonders of ancient Egypt. Meher's father has been guiding tourists through his city for many years. He teaches them about life in busy, modern Egypt, as well as life during the time of the pharaohs.

Tourists often escape the noisy, bustling Cairo streets by taking a trip down the Nile on a felucca.

felucca a small boat powered by sails or oars

What famous landmarks does your country have? How are they different from Egypt's tourist attractions?

Tourist Talk

In Giza, west of Cairo, lies the Great Sphinx. This limestone statue has the body of a lion and the head of a human.

Giza is home to ten pyramids, which were built for the kings. The ancient Egyptians believed that the pyramids were the stepping stones to the sky and the afterworld. Pyramids were usually used as tombs for the kings. There was often a smaller pyramid beside a king's pyramid for the queen's tomb.

Meher's family also trade camels for a living. At the moment, they own twenty-one of them. One day a week, Meher helps his father and older brother at the camel market. The market is filled with the noise of people shouting in an effort to interest buyers in their camels.

Camels have been part of Egyptian culture for hundreds of years. These "ships of the desert" were once regarded as a symbol of importance and wealth. However, camels are also well known for their bad tempers. They bite, spit, and kick, but Meher and his brother move fearlessly among them. They have both grown up around camels and treat them with respect.

Meher and his brother help their father on Friday mornings, as it is the Muslim holy day, so they do not have to go to school. They get up early, because the camel market opens at dawn.

The ancient trade route between western Sudan and southern Egypt is known as the Forty Days Road. This is about how long it took to trek with thousands of camels to the markets in Egypt.

The owners and the buyers of the camels **haggle** over prices. When they have agreed on a price, the camels are loaded onto trucks and taken to their new home.

haggle to bargain over a price

Meher's sister, Latifa, also has a job. She weaves brightly colored wool carpets and tapestries by hand. Her popular Egyptian themes, such as pharaohs, deserts, and feluccas on the Nile, appeal to tourists and other buyers.

Latifa doesn't make carpets all day, however. She works for four hours in the morning at a carpet school, learning the art of carpet making, and then she attends regular school lessons in the afternoon. Latifa's training is sponsored by the Ministry of Education and Egypt's carpet industry. When she completes her education, she will be a highly skilled artist.

Carpet weaving is an ancient art. It takes many years of training to learn how to tie knots and be able to create beautiful, complex carpet designs. Although many young people in Egypt learn how to weave, it is compulsory to attend school until age 14.

Did You Know?

The idea of weaving schools first came from Ramses Wissa Wassef, an Egyptian architect. He wanted to teach children a trade, so he chose the ancient Egyptian art of weaving. In 1953, in the small village of Harrania near Cairo, he worked with nine girls and three boys, teaching them the basics of weaving on simple looms.

Meher's oldest sister, Dalila, sells head scarfs to tourists on weekends.

Meher's father and the other camel drivers meet for a refreshing drink before they set out to guide tourists around the pyramids.

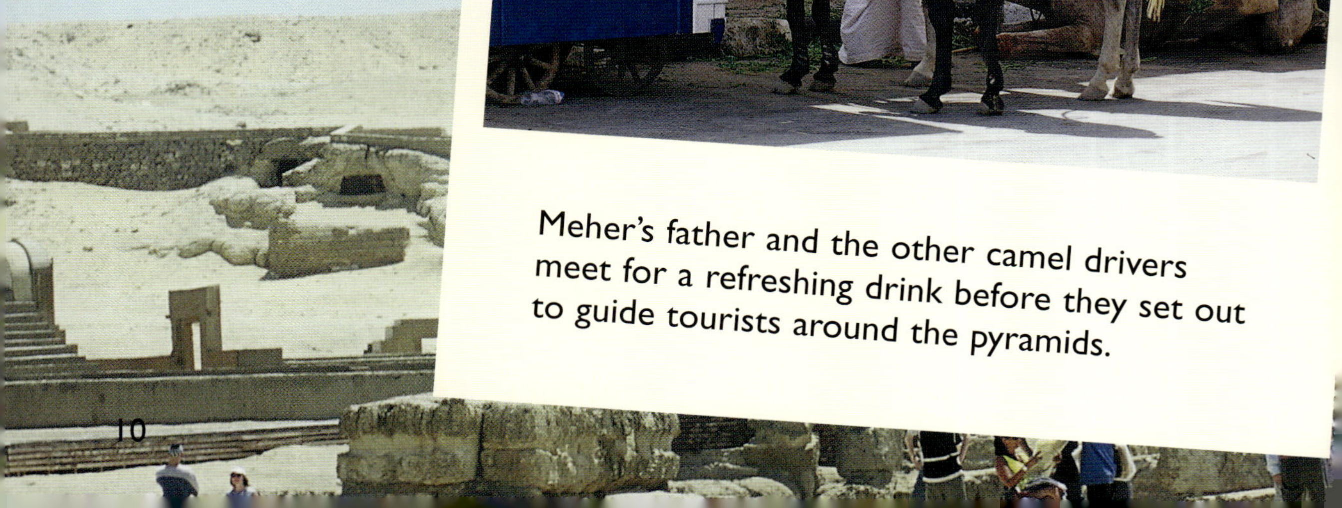

Latifa and her friends like to ride on feluccas.
It is a good way to unwind during their free time.
They like to dance to the music on board.

Going to the market to buy and sell goods is part of the Egyptian culture. It is a common sight to see donkeys pulling carts full of fresh produce along a busy road packed with trucks, buses, and cars. On the side of the road, people sell flat loaves of unleavened bread, and street carts display oranges, which are one of the main crops grown in Egypt. The markets are not only a great place to buy goods, but they are also the perfect meeting place to chat with friends and have a cup of mint tea at one of the many teahouses.

What goods does your country export? What goods does it import?

unleavened flat; made without yeast

Meher's large extended family have been traders for many generations. Meher's cousin, Jahi, learned to make chairs from his father, and he is now very skilled at bending the wood into interesting designs. Jahi and his father sell their products at Khan el-Khalili, a busy market in Old Cairo. It is the oldest market in Egypt.

The Streets of Cairo

Explore Egypt

Egypt lies in the northeast corner of Africa and is mostly desert. Being near sources of water is essential to life in Egypt, as the rainfall is very low. In western Egypt, there are oases scattered in the desert. The people there farm the land, growing crops such as olives and dates.

The Nile River, the longest river in the world, is Egypt's major source of water. Because of the lack of rainwater, many of Egypt's towns and cities are built along the Nile or the Suez Canal, a waterway that links the Red Sea with the Mediterranean Sea. This waterway allows ships to take a shorter route from Europe to Asia without going around the southern tip of Africa.

Suez Canal

oasis an area in a desert where water comes to the surface

Cairo is the capital city of Egypt. The old quarters, the modern parts of the city, and the ancient ruins make this a fascinating place to visit.

On the Go!

What is ancient picture writing called?

Go to page 16

What is the Egyptian name for an outdoor market or bazaar?

Go to page 20

Who started the famous Papyrus Institute?

Go to page 23

Ancient Egypt

Ancient Egypt was one of the world's earliest civilizations and was ruled by powerful kings, called pharaohs. This ancient civilization was very well organized. Skilled workers, such as engineers and architects, helped plan and build magnificent cities, pyramids, and temples.

Early Egyptian society was divided into three main classes. The lower class consisted of peasants and unskilled workers. Craftspeople, merchants, and scribes made up the middle class. The upper class included officials and high priests. A pharaoh ruled all the classes.

The Egyptians invented picture writing known as hieroglyphics. It was the task of the scribes to write the hieroglyphs. They recorded them on clay tablets or papyrus paper.

In ancient Egypt, people lived near the Nile River or close to an oasis.

Moving the Past

These statues of Ramses II, at the Temple of Abu Simbel, were moved when the Aswan Dam was built in the 1960s. The dam would have flooded and destroyed the ruins. Many ancient Egyptian monuments were taken apart and then reassembled on higher ground. The project was coordinated by UNESCO, an international organization.

Modern Egypt

When the pyramids at Giza were built, they were surrounded by desert. Today, the bustling city of Cairo surrounds them. Cities such as Cairo and Alexandria are a mix of old and new. Tall, modern buildings sit next to temples and pyramids that are thousands of years old.

Cairo is both Egypt's largest city and the largest city in Africa. The older parts of the city have narrow streets crammed with old buildings, markets, and hundreds of mosques. The newer sections of Cairo have been carefully designed. Wide streets and public gardens and squares give an impression of space.

mosque a place of worship for people who follow Islam

Does your city or town have old sections? What is the history behind these areas?

Alexandria is the second largest city in Egypt. It is found on the Mediterranean coast and is Egypt's main port. Founded by Alexander the Great in 332 B.C., the city is often referred to as the Pearl of the Mediterranean. Its long, white beaches and warm, sunny climate make it a popular destination for tourists from other countries as well as people from Egypt.

destination a place that someone is going to

Bustling Bazaars

Traditional outdoor markets or bazaars, called *souks*, can be found throughout Egypt. They are usually located in the old parts of the cities. Tourists and locals can wander through workshops and watch craftspeople making brass and copper items, blowing glass, and making hats.

The small, narrow streets in the old market areas twist and turn. Tourists can haggle for Egyptian souvenirs such as paintings done on papyrus paper. Sometimes whole streets are dedicated to selling one kind of item. There are bazaars of just about every variety, including spice bazaars, perfume bazaars, and jewelry bazaars. There is always a stall to look at, but tourists can easily get lost in the crowded markets.

Hatmaker, Khan el-Khalili bazaar

People shop for spices in the Khan el-Khalili bazaar, where spices and other products have been bought and sold since 1382.

How are modern supermarkets or variety stores similar to bazaars?

Museums

People can see treasures from Egypt's past in the museums of Egypt. To prevent the pharaohs' tombs from being robbed in the 1800s, the Egyptian government excavated the tombs and placed the contents in museums. However, many of Egypt's treasures had been sold already to private collectors around the world during the 1700s. Fortunately, many collectors willed their entire collections to museums.

Today, Egyptian treasures can be seen in museums all over the world. In Cairo, the Egyptian Museum exhibits more than 100,000 artifacts. Perhaps its most famous exhibit is one featuring objects from the tomb of King Tutankhamen, who was ancient Egypt's youngest ruler.

Tutankhamen's gold coffin is displayed in a special glass unit. These units are used to display mummies and other precious artifacts. They control the atmosphere to help prevent decay.

Ramses II was a great Egyptian pharaoh. He ordered mighty statues of himself to be built. This limestone statue of the great ruler now lies in a Memphis museum in Egypt.

A Papyrus Museum

The Dr. Ragab Papyrus Institute is a famous tourist attraction. In the 1960s, Dr. Ragab tried to make papyrus paper like the ancient Egyptians. However, the papyrus plant was extinct in Egypt, and the "recipe" for papyrus paper had never been recorded. So Dr. Ragab imported the papyrus plant from Sudan and experimented for four years before successfully making papyrus paper.

What Do You Think?

1. Do you think tourists help keep the old ways and traditions of a country alive?

2. What do you think would happen if a country did not respect its traditions and culture?

Index